NEW ORLEANS TRAVEL GUIDE 2024

Discover The Best Of New Orleans;

Accommodation, What To Do, Sightseeing,

With 3-Days Itinerary For First-Timers

By

Philip S. Ortiz

About The Author

 **Philip S. Ortiz** is a passionate writer specializing in the creation of captivating travel guides. With an unwavering love for exploration and an insatiable curiosity about the world, He has dedicated himself to curating invaluable resources for travellers seeking authentic and immersive experiences.

Drawing upon his extensive personal travels and deep understanding of diverse cultures, he brings a unique perspective to his writing. Through his carefully crafted guidebooks, he aims to transport readers to enchanting destinations, providing them with the knowledge and insights necessary to uncover hidden gems and create unforgettable memories. His travel guides are renowned for their meticulous attention to detail, expert recommendations, and evocative storytelling. By seamlessly blending practical information with captivating narratives, he offers readers a comprehensive and engaging travel companion that goes beyond traditional guidebooks.

Passionate about sharing his love for travel with others, his writing resonates with both seasoned adventurers and armchair travellers alike. His ability to capture the essence of a place and convey its unique charm has earned him a loyal following of wanderlust-driven individuals seeking to embark on their transformative journeys.

With a profound belief in the transformative power of travel, he continues to inspire and guide readers toward remarkable destinations worldwide. Whether it's discovering hidden cultural treasures, immersing oneself in breathtaking landscapes, or engaging with the vibrant tapestry of local life, his travel guides provide the roadmap to unforgettable experiences.

As a writer, he continues to explore the world, unearthing new stories and uncovering the beauty and diversity that lie within each destination. His passion for travel and dedication to his craft shines through in every word, inviting readers to embark on their adventures and create lifelong memories.

So, whether you're a seasoned traveller or an aspiring explorer, Philip S. Ortiz's travel guides are the essential companion to unlock the wonders of the world and embark on a journey of discovery. Get ready to immerse yourself in his expertly crafted narratives and set off on an extraordinary exploration of the globe.

SCAN THE QR CODE BELOW TO SEE OTHER OF MY BOOKS

Table Of Content

Map Of New Orleans

SCAN THE QR CODE BELOW TO VIEW MAP;

Introduction

Embark on an exploration of the effervescent metropolis of New Orleans, a place where the past pirouettes along its avenues, melodies drift through the atmosphere, and the scent of delectable dishes tempts from every direction. Affectionately dubbed the "Big Easy," this distinctive locale on the Mississippi River's edge is a crucible of cultural fusion, a monument to tenacity, and an unparalleled homage to the zest of existence.

In New Orleans, each stone-paved path narrates a saga, and every jazz chord composes an orchestral masterpiece. A locale where the essences of French, African, Spanish, and Creole heritages are entwined, it weaves a cultural mosaic as rich as it is enthralling. Laden with historical significance, the city has withstood tempests, welcomed change, and stands proud with an ethos deeply anchored in its heritage yet receptive to transformation.

Venture into the core of New Orleans and be enveloped by the bewitching ambiance of the French Quarter. Here, historic edifices with ornate ironwork grace the lanes, each turn revealing narratives from an age long gone. From the dynamic thrum of Jackson Square to the spectral allure of St. Louis Cemetery, the French Quarter offers a plethora of visual, auditory, and sensory delights to uncover.

Music forms the lifeblood of New Orleans, with its rhythm resonating citywide. Step into the softly lit confines of jazz establishments where brass and keys reign supreme, or let the heartfelt strains from roadside artists guide you through bustling districts. From the historic Congo Square to the hallowed Preservation Hall, New Orleans beckons you to experience the cadence of its profound musical roots.

Prepare for a gastronomic odyssey unrivalled in its vibrancy. New Orleans is a playground for the palate, where Creole and Cajun essences waltz across your taste buds. Relish the tastes of gumbo, jambalaya, and po'boys, and cap it off with a serving of sugary beignets. Whether dining in a time-honoured eatery or sampling street fare, each meal in New Orleans is a jubilant homage to culinary artistry.

New Orleans is synonymous with festivity, its calendar brimming with colorful festivals and spirited processions. While Mardi Gras shines as an iconic spectacle, the city's year-round festivities immerse you in a whirlwind of cultural, musical, and gastronomic celebrations that embody the city's exuberant soul.

Beyond the city's bustling streets lies a realm of serene beauty. Navigate the Mississippi, delve into enigmatic swamps rich with fauna, or amble through the idyllic Garden District. New Orleans serves as a portal to the splendour of nature and the thrill of open-air escapades.

As you navigate the alluring charms of New Orleans, anticipate the embrace of its inhabitants' warmth. Renowned for their congeniality and graciousness, they are as integral to the city's fabric as its landmarks. Engage with them, share in their dances, and allow them to show you the city's concealed treasures.

In this guide, we extend an invitation to delve into the essence of New Orleans, where each junction is a performance space and every musical note a narrative in a centuries-old tale. Let's embark on an expedition to uncover the history, delight in the tastes, and sway to the rhythm of the Big Easy. Welcome to the journey.

12 Reasons Why You Should Visit New Orleans

In the United States, there is no other city quite like the beautiful city of New Orleans. In spite of the fact that it is known for being a city that is often associated with partying, it is so much more than that.

In the event that you are still trying to persuade yourself, take a look at these top twelve reasons to visit New Orleans, Louisiana.

1. The People

There are a lot of individuals that are pleasant and kind in New Orleans, and they are proud of the place that they call home. They are more than happy to introduce you to the most reputable dining establishments, extend invitations to parties, and maybe even tour you around. In a nutshell, it is a location where you may enjoy genuine friendliness along the Southern coast.

2. The public transit

Streetcars are New Orleans's only advantage, even though the city's public transit system is not as easily accessible as that of other communities. When it comes to transportation inside the city, the streetcars offer an exceptional and one-of-a-kind option.

Ride the St. Charles Avenue Line to view the stunning Southern-style houses or shops on Freret Street and Magazine Street.

Or take the City Park Line out to explore the magnificent City Park, New Orleans Museum of Art, Louisiana Children's Museum, or the New Orleans Botanical Garden.

3. The cuisine

Without a doubt, my top reason to go to New Orleans is the cuisine. The Big Easy's cuisine offers a diverse range of flavors from numerous countries, including low-country boils and beignets as well as French, Creole, and Cajun cuisine. For the tastiest, most genuine food, steer clear of the chain restaurants and visit the smaller establishments.

4. The Cocktail

New Orleans has a thriving cocktail culture in addition to its cuisine. Please don't worry if you don't like partying. This is a fun area of town that doesn't need partying. Spend a day on a cocktail-tasting tour, take a visit to a nearby brewery, or try a locally-made drink. Please use caution while drinking as usual.

5. The Gaming

For some poker or slot action, visit Harrah's, the only casino still operating within the boundaries of New Orleans. Who knows, maybe you'll win enough to go out to a delicious French meal for yourself!

6. The Music

The live music culture in New Orleans is flourishing, especially for jazz and bounce, a distinct kind of hip-hop. Numerous renowned music events take place there as well, including the Voodoo Music + Arts Experience and the New Orleans Jazz Festival.

7. The Construction

From Spanish, French, and Creole influences, to French architecture, Orleans has an abundance of beautiful buildings. Shotgun homes, large Southern plantations, double gallery mansions, and Creole cottages are also seen. Just taking in all of the houses and structures in New Orleans would take up a whole day, if not longer!

8. The Work of Art

Numerous streets in New Orleans are lined with galleries displaying sculptures, paintings, and other works of art. Since there are so many galleries featuring modern and contemporary art, I like the Julia Street neighborhood more. On the other hand, street art is my favorite kind of art in Crescent City. The city is filled with stunning murals and artwork, some of which are by Banksy and Brandon "BMike" Odums of New

Orleans. In addition, you'll be treated to some of the most amazing outdoor decorations you've ever seen if you come around a holiday like Christmas, Halloween, or Mardi Gras.

Imagine beautiful evergreen wreaths and Christmas lights hung with care, enormous beads tastefully placed around porches, homes decked up as Mardi Gras floats, and yards transformed into clever graves. I think that everything is art! You may find it corny, but I find it to be imaginative and enjoyable. That's partially the reason I adore this city.

9. The Magic

With its reputation for the paranormal, New Orleans is home to a good number of fortune tellers, palm readers, tarot card readers, and psychics. It might be entertaining to hear what these perceptive seers have to say, even if you're a skeptic.

10. The Tours

Some cities have packaged and uninspired tours. Not in Louisiana! Numerous excursions are available, including ones that explore graveyards, swamps, mansions, street art, vampire mythology, and much more.

11. The Economy

The calamity that was Hurricane Katrina may have been more than 15 years ago, but its impact is still obvious in many ways. There are still individuals in New Orleans who are displaced, companies devastated, and repairs still required. By pouring money into the economy, you are doing your lot to keep businesses, restaurants, and galleries running and in turn, also keeping people employed.

12. The Museums

New Orleans offers dozens of intriguing and unusual museums to tour, too. A couple of favourites include The Backstreet Cultural Museum and The National World War II Museum.

15 Top-Rated Tourist Attractions In New Orleans

1. The National WWII Museum: The National WWII Museum is the premier tourist attraction in New Orleans, ranking second nationwide. It provides an unforgettable journey through World War II, encompassing domestic industrial efforts and the frontline experiences of American service members. Combining a captivating narrative with poignant personal details, the museum offers immersive exhibits, multimedia encounters, and an extensive array of artifacts and firsthand oral histories. These elements invite visitors to delve into the war's story—its motivations, victories, and contemporary significance. Beyond the galleries, the museum provides exclusive opportunities for hands-on history, including tours and rides on a meticulously restored PT boat, behind-the-scenes access with curators, and exploration of a remarkable collection of restored and functional macro-artifacts. It is operating from early hours; from 8:30 a.m. to 5:00 p.m. Location; 945 Magazine Street, New Orleans, LA 70130-3813.

2. Frenchmen Street: This renowned stretch is renowned as the prime location for the city's premier live music venues, with the Faubourg Marigny area standing out as particularly popular. Location; Frenchmen Street, New Orleans, LA 70116. Open now from 12:00 AM - 11:59 PM.

3. French Quarter: Immerse yourself in the vibrant energy and storied history of the French Quarter, the heart and cultural nucleus of New Orleans. Revel in the lively atmosphere set against stunning colonial architecture, where skilled street performers abound. Explore the city's finest galleries and iconic landmarks, including the magnificent St. Louis Cathedral. Extend your stay into the evening to groove to live jazz in one of the district's renowned clubs. Enhance your experience by joining a food, haunted, or jazz tour led by an insightful local guide. If you plan your visit between February and early March, you can partake in the lively street festivities of Mardi Gras. Open now from 12:00 AM - 11:59 PM.

4. Jackson Square: At the heart of the French Quarter, this historic landmark stands as the city's cultural nucleus, hosting a lively open-air artist colony brimming with vibrancy and activity. Location; 701 Decatur St, New Orleans, LA 70116.

5. Garden District: Once cherished by America's elite, this iconic neighborhood is now the residence of grand historic mansions, unique indie boutiques, and meticulously tended gardens. Location; St Charles Avenue, New Orleans, LA 70130-5968.

6. St. Louis Cathedral: With roots tracing back to 1727, this historic church holds the distinction of being the oldest continuously active cathedral in the U.S. It proudly graces Jackson Square in the heart of the French Quarter. Location; 615 Pere Antoine Aly, New Orleans, LA 70116-3291.

7. New Orleans City Park: City Park, among the largest urban parks in the country, offers a range of recreational activities including golf, tennis, and horseback riding. Location; 1 Palm Dr, New Orleans, LA 70124-4608.

8. Preservation Hall: Founded in 1961, Preservation Hall in New Orleans stands as a tribute to one of America's purest art forms - Traditional New Orleans Jazz. Serving as a music venue, a touring band, and a non-profit organization, Preservation Hall remains committed to its mission as a cornerstone of New Orleans music and culture. Nestled in the heart of the French Quarter on St. Peter Street, the venue hosts intimate, acoustic New Orleans Jazz concerts for over 350 nights a year, showcasing ensembles from a current collective of 100+ local master practitioners. Every night, audiences have the privilege of witnessing the joyful evolution of this venerable and living tradition. Location; 726 St. Peter Street, New Orleans, LA 70116-3182.

9. St. Louis Cemetery No. 1: Established in 1789, this cemetery holds the distinction of being the oldest in New Orleans and is duly recognized on the National Register of Historic Places. Location; 425 Basin St 3421 Esplanade Ave, New Orleans, LA 70112-3535.

10. Blaine Kern's Mardi Gras World: Mardi Gras World stands out as the most distinctive attraction in America's uniquely captivating city. Experience the fascinating process of Mardi Gras creation and get an up-close look at the grandest floats and sculptures that define this iconic celebration. Location; 1380 Port of New Orleans Pl, New Orleans, LA 70130-1805.

11. Royal Street: As one of the oldest streets in the French Quarter of New Oarleans, this historic stretch offers an abundance of exploration opportunities with its curio shops, concept stores, and art galleries. Location; Royal Street, New Orleans, LA 70130.

12. Basin St. Station: Welcoming a multitude of visitors daily to New Orleans, Basin St. Station serves as an authentic and captivating introduction to our culturally diverse and historically rich city. The first floor hosts a staffed visitor information center featuring informative community exhibits, a performance venue, a walking tour kiosk, and a genuinely New Orleans and Louisiana-themed gift shop.

Nestled in the lobby of Basin St. Station Welcome Center, the Basin St. Cafe, a French Market-style grab-n-go New Orleans coffee bar operated by Messina's, adds to the experience. For breathtaking views overlooking the French Quarter, The Rooftop on Basin, a special event space atop Basin St. Station, is available. The salon and terrace spaces provide guests with a unique blend of New Orleans charm, combining traditional elements with an elegant and chic style. Location; 501 Basin St, New Orleans, LA 70112-3552.

13. Hermann-Grima House: This meticulously restored French Quarter residence, constructed in 1831, showcases a Federalist architectural façade, an original operational open-hearth kitchen, urban slave quarters, and an expansive courtyard. The Urban Enslavement Tour at

Hermann-Grima House delves into the experiences of those who were enslaved in an urban setting, highlighting the distinctions from those in rural settings and emphasizing how the contributions of individuals of African descent have profoundly shaped New Orleans. Voted by Condé Nast Traveler as one of the best tours in New Orleans and the sole tour listed from a museum, the tour offers a unique perspective. The Hermann-Grima House team believes that nothing conveys a story quite like a home. Furthermore, the property's 19th-century carriage house is the home of The Exchange Shop, originally established in 1881 by The Woman's Exchange and recognized as one of the oldest women-led non-profits in the South. Location; 820 Saint Louis St, New Orleans, LA 70112-3416.

14. The Sazerac House: The Sazerac House offers a unique blend of one-part history and traditions, and two-part interactive exhibits and experiences, seasoned with spirited events and a dash of rich New Orleans culture. Come visit to indulge in distinctive tastes and traditions that are worth cherishing. Here, the past, present, and future converge, all while savoring cocktails. (*Holiday and parade hours are subject to change.). Location; 101 Magazine St, New Orleans, LA 70130-2420.

15. Audubon Zoo: Nestled in historic Uptown New Orleans, Audubon Zoo presents an exotic array of animals from around the world, complemented by engaging educational programs, hands-on animal encounters, and vibrant gardens. The zoo's unique natural habitat exhibits, including the award-winning Louisiana

Swamp and Jaguar Jungle, highlight the intricate relationship between humans and nature. Be sure not to miss the daily animal presentations, chats, and feeds, featuring highly endangered species such as whooping cranes, Amur leopards, orangutans, a white tiger, and mysterious white alligators. Audubon Zoo consistently ranks among the country's best for its innovative exhibits and entertainment value!

Entry Requirements & Customs in New Orleans

Passports

- All individuals flying into the U.S., regardless of citizenship, must present a valid passport.
- U.S. and Canadian citizens entering from the Western Hemisphere should adhere to the Western Hemisphere Travel Initiative (WHTI) for potential additional document requirements.
- Children aged 15 and below can enter with a U.S. birth certificate or alternative proof of U.S. citizenship.

Passport Information for select countries

- Australia: Reach out to the Australian Passport Information Service (www.passports.gov.au).

- Canada: Refer to the Passport Office, Department of Foreign Affairs and International Trade (www.ppt.gc.ca).

- Ireland: For passport inquiries, contact the Passport Office, Setanta Centre, Molesworth Street, Dublin 2 (www.foreignaffairs.gov.ie).

- New Zealand: Check with the Passports Office, Department of Internal Affairs, Wellington (www.passports.govt.nz).

- United Kingdom: Seek assistance from the Identity and Passport Service (www.ips.gov.uk).

For U.S. citizens

- Access regional passport office details through the U.S. State Department website or contact the National Passport Information Center.

Visas

- The Visa Waiver Program (VWP) permits citizens from specific countries to enter the U.S. for up to 90 days without a visa.

- Travellers from VWP nations should register online via the Electronic System for Travel Authorization (ESTA) before departure.

- Citizens of other countries may require a valid passport, and a tourist visa, and must fulfil specific criteria.

For U.S. Visa information

- Refer to http://travel.state.gov or consult the relevant U.S. Embassy/Consulate.

Customs

- For U.S. Customs details, consult the closest U.S. embassy/consulate or visit www.cbp.gov.

New Orleans Travel Guide 2024| Philp S. Ortiz

- Verify allowed items when returning home through the respective agencies.

Customs Contacts

- <u>U.S. Citizens:</u> Obtain information from U.S. Customs & Border Protection (www.cbp.gov).
- <u>Canadian Citizens:</u> Check with the Canada Border Services Agency (www.cbsa-asfc.gc.ca).
- <u>U.K. Citizens:</u> Inquire with HM Customs & Excise (www.hmce.gov.uk).
- <u>Australian Citizens:</u> Refer to the Australian Customs Service (www.customs.gov.au).
- <u>New Zealand Citizens:</u> Seek guidance from New Zealand Customs (www.customs.govt.nz).

Medical Requirements

- Unless arriving from an epidemic-affected region, no specific inoculations or vaccinations are mandated for entry into the United States.

New Orleans Travel Cost

Among all the world's major cities, New Orleans has a mystique all its own. It's a place you won't soon forget because of its flawless fusion of world cuisines, conflicting cultures, and eerie past, all perfectly seasoned with its Southern charm. I mean, I'll never forget my week-long vacation to New Orleans, which included walks under the massive live oaks, crawfish feasts, and lovely cable car rides in addition to the city's top attractions.

It's hardly feasible to spend enough time in New Orleans to sample every mouthwatering beignet and hear every terrifying tale, but a week will get you started. The fact that New Orleans was once the capital city and the center of French

Louisiana before it was acquired by the United States contributes to some of its grandeur. Being one of the most haunted towns in the US, it was founded in 1718 and has had its fair share of tragedy and loss.

This one's for you if you're a ghost fan. New Orleans is also for you if your preferences are for eating out, fishing excursions, strolling tours, and very, really, (really) amazing donuts.

Best of all, you can do it on a tight budget! Here's a helpful look at how to budget for an incredible vacation – let us be your guide!

Average Trip to New Orleans Cost in 2024

The cost of a vacation to New Orleans for two persons with an average duration of one week is around $2,700:

- Generally speaking, the cost of lodging is $75 per night.
- The typical cost of a flight is $300 per passenger.
- Expenses for food, drink, and activities totaling one hundred dollars.
- Transportation: a total of one hundred dollars
- $2,700 is the total cost.

The city of New Orleans is a holiday destination that is quite economical, as you can see. There is a great deal to see, but the majority of the things that make it remarkable are free. You will not be required to pay high admission fees, and this is in contrast to other wonderful tourist places such as Disneyland. And in contrast to other renowned cities with wonderful culture, architecture, and nightlife (think New York or LA), you won't pay a large cost-of-living charge merely for being there. Instead, New Orleans is the right blend of awe-inspiring and inexpensive. You may travel with one other person or a group – or even by yourself – and complete a full trip diary in a single week. Between the stores and the restaurants, the architecture and the walking tours, the nightlife and the breezy morning coffees, it's an ideal holiday right in our neighborhood.

New Orleans Trip Cost: Average by Item

When you are making plans for your vacation, it is only normal that you would want to know how much it would cost. It is important to keep in mind that the costs shown here are all averages; thus, you should not put your faith in any particular estimate until you have searched the internet and discovered the best offer for yourself.

However, the data that are shown here are rather trustworthy. Please make sure that you take into consideration major holidays and festivals since these events have the potential to significantly raise the cost of hotels and flights during certain periods.

Costs of Lodging and Meals

If you know where to search, you may find a pretty comfortable place to stay in New Orleans for about $75 and $80 per night for a typical couple. When looking for hotels that are within your price range, you may want to consider staying at the Le Méridien, the Voco St. James Hotel, or the Hilton New Orleans Riverside. Think about staying at a hostel if you want to save even more money. You can bring costs down to approximately $30 per night, which will give you more money to spend on crawfish, beignets, and the finest coffee you'll ever taste. Younger travelers often don't mind having less space; they also don't mind sharing restrooms.

Word to the wise … The purchase of a package that includes airline and hotel accommodations may make a trip to many locations in the United States more cost-effective; however, this is not the case with New Orleans. Flight expenses are so affordable, and you save enough money sharing a hotel with your travelling buddy, that you won't realise large savings by purchasing a package. Most likely all you'll do is restrict your alternatives.

Overall, if you're not finicky and prepared to stay in a 3-star hotel, $75 a night is fine so long as you book early and don't travel during holiday festivities. Even during Mardi Gras –

which is when I visited – there was a selection of reasonable hotels if you prepared beforehand.

Flight Costs

I've got some wonderful news. Getting to New Orleans is as economical as staying there! A round-trip ticket from LA to New Orleans will only cost you roughly $150 on average, less if you're a consummate bargain hunter. And, as I constantly advise folks, if you shop airfares in incognito mode so that browsers don't know you've searched that region previously and boost the costs on you … sure, it's a thing.

From New York City, it's a touch more costly, approximately $275 per person on average. From a smaller international airport that's not a hub, such as Portland, Oregon, you'll spend around the same. If you're flying out of a rural airport, throw on $100 or more. On the other side, if you're flying from the South, you'll pay nearly nothing. On average, you can pay approximately $300 for a round-trip airfare and get there from anywhere in the nation.

Food, Drink & Activity Costs

The amount you spend in New Orleans is determined on what you want to accomplish there. If you're the sort who travels to tie one on, then you should expect to spend buckets.

Canal Street; the major avenue for drinkers – is spendy. So are other pubs and restaurants in fashionable or popular locations. Plan to pay roughly $10 for a drink, however, if you avail yourself of happy hours and discounts, you may of course save money.

Street food, luckily, is relatively affordable. The po'boy is a favourite of mine — French bread loaded with fried fish, pickles, and vegetables. You can also find crawfish on the street, tacos, and virtually anything else ever created on Earth. Save your finances for a couple of great meals while you're there - roughly $50 a dish – to obtain an elite eating experience.

As indicated above, New Orleans is a genuinely great city to experience without spending a dollar. It features plenty of magnificent chichi neighborhoods, such as the Garden District, Lake Terrace and Oaks, and Lake Shore. Plan to board a bus to the region to do some strolling and sightseeing, and you could even spy on a celebrity. Being particularly fond of colleges, I also explored Loyola and Tulane.

They are a magnificent jumble of architectural types placed between manicured lawns and gorgeous landscaping, with palm palms blowing in the wind. If you, like me, prefer a nice stroll about a campus, you won't be disappointed — and like any other college, they're free to go around.

If you're the sort that has to visit the fee-charging attractions, then you definitely must acquire a Go City pass. For $74 a day, you can get into a ton of the city's top attractions, from the Paddlewheeler Creole Queen Cruise to the Long Vue House and Gardens to different cemeteries and voodoo excursions. Just be sure to arrange this day wisely so you can completely exploit the expense savings.

Overall, aim to spend $100 per person every day. New Orleans boasts a top-notch public transportation system that's both affordable and reliable. You can snag a Jazzy Pass at just $3 for a single day, $8 for a trio of days, or $15 for an entire week. If you prefer, there's also the option of a one-off bus fare for $1.25. Given the unlimited access the pass provides, it's a steal for both day and night travel.

Even taxis won't break the bank. As the city's website notes, New Orleans may be a big city, but it feels small when it comes to cab fares. Zipping across town in a taxi, say from a French Quarter hotel to an Uptown jazz haunt or a local dining spot, typically sets you back less than $20. And if you're coming straight from the airport to the downtown area, expect to pay around $36 for one or two people, or $15 each if you're a group of three or more.

In essence, getting around won't eat into your time or wallet. A couple could easily keep their week's transportation expenses under $100 with a Jazzy Pass each, a handful of taxi rides, and some good old-fashioned footwork.

Backpacking New Orleans Suggested Budgets

Lodging for Backpackers in New Orleans

Hostels in New Orleans are very affordable and, considering the city's notorious image, a fantastic place to meet new people. In New Orleans, many hostels have a strong social component and may become rather boisterous at times. Hopefully, you're not the shy person who stays in the dorms.

Remember that New Orleans is a tourist destination, and destinations of this kind are supposed to have an abundance of lodging! Beyond mere hostels, New Orleans offers a wide variety of lodges, from quirky bungalows to the most luxurious penthouse suites, as well as eco-friendly accommodations. You have the option!

For the most part, I like Airbnb in New Orleans. There are several possibilities in New Orleans for all types of travelers, and they are friendlier and cozier than hotels! There are some amazing Louisiana cabins in the French Quarter and the countryside outside of the city if you're a nature lover.

Check out VRBO, Airbnb's main rival, for even more options when it comes to lodging. Vacation rentals with personalities, such as VRBOs in New Orleans, are ideal for a trip to one of the most unusual places in the US.

For those on a tight budget, there are many RV parks and campsites in New Orleans that are located inside the city boundaries. Just don't forget to bring a good hiking tent and secure your vehicle!

Cheap Lodging Strategies in New Orleans

I understand the urge to have a roof over your head sometimes. At other times, you're exerting every effort to save pennies on pennies. It may be time to stay someplace else than a hostel if you're attempting to save money on your trip to New Orleans. Furthermore, it could be difficult to locate a hotel on Bourbon Street that isn't quite expensive. Try one of these if you need to save costs:

1. Couchsurfing is the greatest method to save money on lodging since you can usually crash

for free when you do it. Another fantastic way to see hidden New Orleans and get a more genuine taste of the city is to stay with a local host.

2. Make use of your backpacking network—you never know who may be your buddy in a new place! You could have met someone from New Orleans or know someone who knows someone if you've traveled a lot.

3. Camp! - A rising trend in many cities is urban camping. These are affordable, safe, friendly, and cozy campgrounds. They are also often calmer since they are situated on the outskirts of the town.

Costs of Backpacking in New Orleans

Because New Orleans is a very seasonal town, costs may vary significantly based on when you come. Come during the Mardi Gras festivities, and bring plenty of cash. But trips to New Orleans may be quite affordable in the off-peak times. There are always methods to save expenses and travel with less money, no matter whether you are organizing a vacation to New Orleans. It's essential to have some inexpensive travel advice if you want to prolong your vacation and visit anywhere in the USA on the cheap.

I've become rather adept at keeping my trip expenditures to a minimum. I'm going to provide my greatest travel advice about New Orleans here, some of which took me years to master. No matter the season, you may go to New Orleans on a budget by using the recommendations in this book.

For New Orleans, a smaller daily budget might be in the range of $50 to $60. You may use this to obtain a dorm bed, food, bus passes, and additional cash for drinks or other purchases. Your biggest outlay in New Orleans will be your lodging. In the summer and autumn, hotels in New Orleans may be found at reasonable costs; however, beware of the spring months, when rates spike from February to May.

If you want to save as much money as possible on housing in New Orleans, consider staying at one of the city's hostels, campsites, or eco-lodges. You can very much choose your food price. In the Garden District, how about French cuisine with a Michelin star? I wish you luck in comprehending that law. If you're on a tight budget, you're best off sticking to street gumbo or dining at one of the food halls.

As always, keep an eye on how much you consume. Insensitivity may have a serious toll on your finances.

A Day-to-Day Budget in New Orleans

This is a summary of a typical New Orleans daily budget that includes the average cost of each expenditure!

Expense	Broke Backpacker	Frugal Traveller	Creature of Comfort
Accommodation	$0-$30	$30-$80	$80+
Food	$15-$20	$20-$30	$30+
Transport	$0-$3	$3-$10	$10+
Nightlife	$0-$10	$10-$40	$40+
Activities	$0-10	$10-$20	$20+

Total	$15-$73	$73-$180	$180+

Some Free Activities in New Orleans

Making the most of all the free events in New Orleans is the ideal way to go there on a tight budget. Enjoy yourself; some of the best things to do in New Orleans are completely free as well!

1. **Movies:** Outdoor movie screenings are quite popular in New Orleans. These are often free to see and take place in public areas like parks. Don't miss Rivertown Movies in the Park, Cinema Sundays in the French Quarter, and the Moonlight Movies series.

2. **Free museums:** Several cultural institutions in New Orleans provide free admission on

certain days of the week or year. These include the World War II Museum, the House of Dance and Feathers, the Historic New Orleans Collection, and the Newcomb Art Gallery. Free days are available at the Ogden Museum and Art Museum, but only for residents of Louisiana.

3. **Concerts and jam sessions:** music can be heard all around this city, and it's sometimes completely free! New Orleans has several free performances all year long, including Jazz in the Park and Wednesdays at the Square. Every second Wednesday, the local Bon Operatit also offers free opera performances. There's always a street performer nearby to serenade you if they don't work out.

4. **Comedy shows:** There are free events held every week in New Orleans' thriving comedy

clubs. Among the activities are improv sessions, seminars, and open mics. You may have to purchase a drink at the bar, and we advise you to do so since seeming frugal makes you an obvious target for jokes.

5. **The better things:** Free guided tours of several local breweries in New Orleans are available. Participants get free beer from NOLA Brewing! From 10 a.m. to 10 p.m., the New Orleans Cigar Factory also provides facility tours. It's OK to smoke.

Budget-Friendly Travel Advice for New Orleans

Try one of these cost-cutting strategies if you're seeking more inexpensive ways to explore New Orleans!

- Take note of the guest discounts available on the official website of New Orleans! Get further savings by printing out the sheet.

- The three-martini lunch is a practice that dates back to a period when being wasted throughout the day was considered socially acceptable. However, these days, it's largely associated with fantastic drink specials. Martinis at certain New Orleans restaurants may be had for as little as $0.25! This stuff is very risky.

- Cheap or even free oysters Making use of the many oyster specials available across the city is among the least expensive things to do in New Orleans. These may be purchased for less than $0.50 per shellfish. At Le Bon Temps Roule, they're even free on Fridays!

- Eat at the neighborhood restaurants: New Orleans is known for its excellent food scene, but dining at five-star establishments or in tourist neighborhoods can spoil your experience. Visit a greasy spoon cafe or go to a dive bar sometimes and eat the house gumbo.

- Happy hour: If the complimentary oysters and quarter martinis haven't won you over, there are many more deals in the area. Happy Hours in New Orleans are insane. You'll undoubtedly discover something if you just go about the city between 4 and 6 p.m.

- Make as many meals at home as you can. Purchasing your groceries and cooking at home is one of the most effective methods to save a ton of money for travelers.

Best Time To Travel To New Orleans

Because New Orleans is subject to a wide range of events and weather seasons, there is unquestionably a certain time of year that is ideal for a visit. Those who are not fans of mass tourism should steer clear of the Mardi Gras season.

The Springtime

If you are not concerned about the cost of your trip to New Orleans, then the months of February through May are without a doubt the finest time to go. New Orleans has a quiet weather pattern with temperatures that are nice at this time of year.

In addition, this is the year when the most exciting celebrations in New Orleans take place, such as Mardi Gras, French Quarter Fest, and Jazz Fest celebrations. The prices, on the other hand, will be completely absurd throughout these months. It is expected that the majority of accommodations, including hotels, Airbnb, and even cardboard boxes, will be reserved many months in advance.

As a result of this, a significant number of New Orleans's local businesses and attractions are closed during the celebration of Mardi Gras. There is a possibility that you might be better off waiting till everything has gone if you are not expressly planning on visiting New Orleans for this occasion.

Summer

As June arrives, so does the rain, humidity, and sultry heat. During the summer season (June-September) the city might seem desolate at times since barely any visitors arrive for fear of the heat or storms. As such, you can get some amazing bargains on hotels during this period.

Visiting during the summer might be a more real New Orleans experience. The city is undoubtedly teeming with visitors and several highly major events, including ESSENCE and Satchmo, happen this season as well.

August and September are peak storm months, which is normally a bleak period for New Orleans. These storms may wreak havoc on the metropolis and are frequently dealt with with a high degree of seriousness. If a large storm is on the way, don't be shocked to see shops boarded up and shut down.

Fall

October- December is post-hurricane season and much like spring, it's arguably the finest time of year to travel to New Orleans since the weather will still be beautiful and there will be fewer people than in the spring months.

Winter

December-February is the coldest month of the year in NOLA, however, they still tend to be significantly warmer than the rest of the mainland United States. Don't expect to encounter many travellers at this time, and be prepared for changing temperatures. You may also feel confident that your chances of witnessing a storm will be really minimal.

Staying Safe in New Orleans

Following Hurricane Katrina, there was a slight decline in safety in New Orleans. After the devastating storm destroyed whole neighbourhoods and villages, New Orleans was reduced to a wasteland. The result was a generalized disruption, a scarcity of food, and a greater reliance on public assistance.

The city became more lawless over time. The miserable people who continued to reside in New Orleans were forced to do criminal actions to survive, making the city seem like a kind of purgatory. There was murder, robbery, and looting. Chronic criminality persisted in the city even after it began to recover.

New Orleans is not the chaotic mess it was after Katrina; instead, it has reverted to much of its previous character. Nearly every tourist destination in New Orleans is welcoming and safe for visitors. Even yet, New Orleans continues to rank among the riskiest cities in the nation. Even Nevertheless, the outside regions, which tourists should find of little interest, are where the majority of the violence occurs.

Make sure you verify these locations' status with the local authorities before you even consider approaching them. You can find yourself in peril if you go into one of these areas at random. You must always use common sense when it comes to safety while visiting New Orleans, no matter where you are. There are still pickpockets and con artists who wait to take advantage of tourists in popular areas.

New Orleans's Rock 'n' Roll, Drugs, and Sex

Many believe that the best place to party in the United States is New Orleans; it makes going to Las Vegas seem like a kid's party. You'll probably want to get lit at least once while visiting the Big Easy because of its renowned Mardi Gras, colorful people, and regular opportunities for revelry.

In Louisiana, alcohol is allowed, but other than that, you can find anything and anything in the city if you know where to look. Be very careful about who you buy from if you want to indulge in drug tourism in New Orleans. It's common knowledge that dealers will cut their losses and sell to tourists who know what. Do not in headfirst; instead, wait until you are with a knowledgeable local who is aware of the differences.

There are several strip clubs and other adult entertainment venues in New Orleans. Whether you want to partake in this or have sex while driving, make sure you treat others with respect and use safe sexual practices.

Before Travelling To New Orleans, Get Insurance

In New Orleans, it might be dangerous to travel without insurance. particularly in light of the well-known (and ludicrous) for-profit healthcare system in the USA. Therefore, before you go on a vacation, you should think about getting good travel insurance. I have been using World Nomads for a while now, and throughout that time, I have made a few claims. They're expert, reasonably priced, and easy to use. It would even be handy for them to let you buy or renew a policy after you've left on your trip and are abroad. Make sure you get backpacker insurance well in advance of your trip. In that sense, there are many options, but Safety Wing is a wise place to start. They provide the exact kind of insurance that long-term travellers and digital nomads require: month-to-month payments, no lock-in contracts, and no itinerary requirements.

How to Get Into and Around New Orleans

New Orleans has one major airport that handles most of its air traffic – Louis Armstrong International Airport. The airport is located quite close to the city but getting to and from is not as easy as it should be. The airport is a quick 20-minute drive away from the French Quarter but costs a minimum of $35, Uber or taxi. If that sounds like a bit much to you, that's because it is. Those who want to travel cheaply to the city centre from Louis Armstrong can use the E-2 bus, which stops on the second floor. Travel time is 45 minutes.

New Orleans Travel Guide 2024| Philp S. Ortiz

There are numerous Amtrak trains and mainliner bus companies offering services to New Orleans. Union Passenger Terminal is the primary arrival/departure port for all of these. Visiting New Orleans with a car is a relatively straightforward task. I-10 is the main highway in and out of New Orleans and it runs right through the heart of the city.

When driving in the city centre just be aware of where you park – parking metres can be expensive and carjackings are on the rise. When you're ready to leave New Orleans, there are plenty of onward destinations. A sunny Florida road trip is a good choice if you're living the vanlife. Just be aware that the South is a pretty big region and that drive times can be longer than you think. Refer below for a list of Southern cities and their distances.

Baton Rouge (LA) – 1.5 hours

Mobile (AL) – 2 hours

Tallahassee (FL) – 5.5 hours

Houston (TX) – 5.5 hours

Memphis (TN) – 5.5 hours

Atlanta (GA) – 6.5 hours

Dallas (TX) – > 8 hours

Getting Around New Orleans

Once you can wrap your head around the weird layout, New Orleans is actually relatively easy to get around. New Orleans is pretty fun to walk in and the public transport is good enough that you can go just about anywhere you need to. The city itself is shaped like a crescent and tends to disorientate those who are not used to its odd shape. Cardinal directions seemingly don't exist in New Orleans, which is a phenomenon you can test out simply by asking a local which way is north. (They'll look at you like you're crazy.)

The best way to navigate New Orleans is to just refer to major landmarks in the city. If you ask for directions, you will often be told to just "head towards the river" or "the lake." Figure out where these places are at all times, and you'll be golden. Thanks to its overwhelming array of shopping streets, one of the most fun things to do in New Orleans is to just walk around.

You could spend an entire afternoon just browsing around the likes of Magazine Street, Freret Street, or Royal Street, and you wouldn't be wasting your time.

New Orleans has several historic trams that are as useful as they are enjoyable. The streetcars themselves resemble their European cousins and could fit right in Milan or Lisbon.

There are two streetcar lines: red for Canal Street and green for St Charles. Both are major throughways and can get quite busy. New Orleans has a public transport system, referred to as RTA. There are plenty of buses running throughout the city. Rides cost $1.25 one way or $3 for an entire day.

Perfect Itinerary In New Orleans For First-Timers

Once you arrive in the Big Easy, there is a very strong possibility that you will not want to leave. This is because the Big Easy is so incredible. The overwhelming quantity of mouthwatering cuisine, entertaining live music, and stunning architecture are likely to leave the office majority of tourists feeling impressed.

Therefore, while it is possible to spend a lifetime getting to know New Orleans, the ideal length of time to begin planning a trip to New Orleans is three days. This will give you the opportunity to see all of the well-known sights in the city, satisfy your cravings for creole and cajun cuisine, and even go off the beaten path for a little while.

<u>Day one of the New Orleans itinerary includes visits to the French Quarter and the Bywater.</u>
This New Orleans travel guide is going to begin with the touristic things, so let's get that out of the way right away. The French Quarter is going to be your first stop today, and after that, you are going to make your way to Marigny/Bywater.

Let's begin our exploration in the French Quarter. The French were the ones who first constructed this section of the city, which is the oldest portion of the city. Not only is the bulk of the architecture in this area not French, but the majority of the modern architecture in the Quarter is Spanish. This is an interesting fact.

Many of the attractions that are considered to be must-sees in New Orleans may be found in the French Quarter. Two of the most notorious neighbourhoods in the world, Bourbon Street and Jackson Square, may be found in this area. It is possible to spend a considerable amount of time in Jackson just observing passing individuals.

In the vicinity of Jackson Square, there are a variety of exciting places to visit. First, stop by The Cabildo–a museum devoted to New Orleans' origins– while Preservation Hall is one of the most famous Jazz sites in the city. The French Quarter offers several of the most renowned restaurants in New Orleans as well as some great locations to shop. Be sure to go by the French Market, a flea market of sorts that's been operating since 1791. End your stay in the

Big Easy's most renowned neighborhood with a short (or not so fast) stop at the Old Absinthe House for a Sazerac.

When you're ready to escape the crowds, travel toward Marigny and Bywater. These are two small communities in New Orleans and are more laid back. If you stroll along Royal Street, you'll get to pass the Lalaurie Mansion, Palace French Market, and Studio Be. Royal Street itself is quite boutique so you'll get to window shop a lot. End your day with a drink at Bacchanal Spirits and a performance at Music Box Village.

<u>Day 2 of the New Orleans itinerary: Feel the vibes of City Park and Lakeview</u>
On the second day of our New Orleans travel guide, go near the lake for a day of relative peace. You'll be spending a lot of time in the

park and touring New Orleans' numerous spectacular cemeteries. From the French Quarter, board the Canal Street Streetcar and ride it till the end of the line. First, you'll rocket through the crowded city center. As you cross beneath the I-10, you'll notice the first of the day's mausoleums on the right: St. Louis Cemetery. Hop off if you like or push on.

After around 20 minutes, you should reach the end of the streetcar. Directly in front of you should lie two more of the city's most affluent cemeteries: Metairie and Greenwood. Wander around these necropolises and see the numerous beautiful headstones and metal embellishments. Just please be courteous of offerings and Holy Ground, if there are any.

Just up from the cemeteries is the massive New Orleans City Park, which is where we're headed next. This park is a fantastic location to sit and watch the clouds go past.

You'll be travelling among gigantic oaks and cypresses that are covered with one of New Orleans' most recognized features: Spanish Moss AKA "Old Man Beard." The trees moan and the moss moves from the breeze, the most calm moments you'll experience in the city. If you visit the Singing Oak near the Art Museum, you'll get the opportunity to hear its music fashioned by a handful of bespoke wind chimes.

When you're ready, travel back to the city centre via Esplanade Avenue or continue up towards Harrison. Harrison is the major street in the residential Lakeview area and features a variety of nice pubs and restaurants.

The third day of the New Orleans itinerary is spent traveling from St. Charles to Audubon

Let's begin our exploration of Lee Circle, which is home to two museums that we have not yet visited: the National World War II Museum and the Ogden Museum. In particular, the Ogden is worth visiting because it houses a collection of historical Southern art, which frequently addresses difficult topics such as colonialism and slavery.

Starting from this point forward, the St. Charles Streetcar is going to serve as our primary mode of transportation. You will be traveling through and near several of New Orleans's most desirable neighborhoods, so you should get ready to hop on and off. Both Freret Street and Magazine Street are very pleasant places to stroll around, and they are situated a couple of blocks on either side of St. Charles Avenue. There is a possibility that you could walk down one and then return via the other, but doing so would require a significant amount of walking.

Oretha Castle Haley Boulevard (OCH), which is on the verge of becoming the next major pedestrian street, is located near Lee Circle. Stop by this little slice of New Orleans if you want to get a glimpse of the city before it is absorbed into the matrix of mass consumption. Eventually, you'll reach the Garden District further on. This area is home to numerous stately mansions from bygone eras as well as several magnificent oak trees. This is also where Lafayette Cemetery is located, and it's possibly the coolest in the city.

For me, Audubon Park is where it ends. You'll see Tulane to your right as you step off the tram. Public access is available to the on-campus Newcomb Art Museum.

More Time Spent in New Orleans?

Of course, New Orleans can supply more for the leisurely set. Though you could easily spend months here and not grow bored, the city offers enough activities to keep you occupied for at least a week. The following are a few lesser-known activities in New Orleans:

Take a trip down the Mississippi River on the only real steamboat in New Orleans, the Steamboat Natchez. As you cruise along the water, you'll not only get to enjoy a gentle breeze, but because this is the Big Easy, live New Orleans jazz music is guaranteed.

<u>Visit Mardi Gras World:</u> Open seven days a week, Mardi Gras World offers an inside look at one of the most amazing festivals globally. Discover the event's history and the creation process of the recognizable floats!

<u>Visit Marie Laveau's Voodoo House:</u> Discover the practice that is ingrained in the history and culture of the city by visiting this museum and store, which is housed in the former residence of the Scond Voodoo Queen of New Orleans. Shop the windows, get a psychic reading, or pick up a memento at this distinctly New Orleans establishment.

<u>See the St. Louis Cathedral:</u> This historic church, which was built in the 1700s, is the oldest Catholic cathedral in the continental United States and a great place to find some peace in Jackson Square.

<u>Take a Bike Tour:</u> Riding a bike is one of the best ways to see New Orleans! Indeed, a self-guided or group tour is a great way to see all of the city's most famous sights. The city is surprisingly bike friendly.

Do's And Don'ts In New Orleans

When you picture New Orleans, images of Mardi Gras, lively scenes on Bourbon Street, and the distinctive shout of "N'awlins" by the locals might spring to mind.

However, the city has so much more to offer than what meets the eye for newcomers setting foot in the Big Easy. It's impossible to experience everything, but your itinerary could be packed with riverboat rides, bayou tours, and a plethora of museums and eateries.

If you're just beginning to explore, Here's a list of five must-dos for your inaugural trip to the city – plus five activities you might consider skipping.

Actions to Take When Visiting New Orleans

1. Definitely indulge in the local cuisine. Dive into a world of flavors with New Orleans' famous po'boys, muffalettas, and beignets. Embark on a culinary tour to sample the best of both Creole and Cajun delights. Remember, a trip to Cafe du Monde for their legendary beignets is practically a rite of passage!

2. Make time for some eerie adventures. If you're up for it, New Orleans offers a spine-tingling experience with ghost tours, voodoo shops, and even vampire boutiques. Get a taste of the Southern Gothic atmosphere, and maybe catch "The Skeleton Key" or the initial seasons of "True Blood" for some pre-trip chills.

3. Experience the vibrant nightlife of Frenchmen Street. Let the rhythms of jazz, blues, and rock lead you on a merry dance from one lively music venue to another. It's the perfect way to immerse yourself in the city's rich musical heritage.

4. Take a leisurely stroll through the Garden District. While the French Quarter boasts incredible architecture, the Garden District is not to be missed. As the folks at Pack Up + Go say, you'll wander past grand mansions and beautifully kept gardens in this picturesque part of town.

5. Seek out a prime spot to admire the Mississippi River. Amidst all the urban exploration, take a moment to soak in the views of this mighty river. Near Jackson Square, you can enjoy a stunning panorama with the river on one side and the majestic St. Louis Cathedral on the other.

What you can skip to do in New Orleans

1. Avoid making plans to spend your entire evening on Bourbon Street. It's a vibrant and notorious hotspot in the French Quarter, teeming with party-goers, but it's not necessarily the place to linger all night. Swing by earlier when it's calmer, especially if you're not into the party scene. And for those who are, remember to stay safe and keep an eye on your surroundings.

2. Don't let the sun dominate your day. New Orleans is known for its blistering heat and sudden heavy rains during the summer. If you find yourself overheating, make sure to carve out some time to cool down, whether that's at a pool or a spot with good air conditioning.

3. Resist the urge to have your palm read by the first fortune-teller you come across. It's your life, and if palm reading is on your agenda, go for it. Just remember, there are plenty of options out there, so take a moment to research before you choose a random vendor on the street.

4. Hold off on visiting Cafe du Monde as soon as you wake up. The experience is definitely worth it, but consider going when it's less busy at night. That way, you can savor those delicious, powdered-sugar beignets without the crowds.

5. If you're not into spicy cuisine, steer clear of it. New Orleans offers a plethora of fiery foods and sauces, like the ones at Pepper Palace that require a waiver just to taste. If the thought of that doesn't excite you, there's no point in pushing your limits just for the sake of it.

New Orleans Customs and Traditions

New Orleans brims with captivating customs that originate from its European and Afro-Caribbean heritage. A number of these practices arose simply because they were practical, like the habit of having red beans and rice on Mondays.

Meanwhile, many are deeply anchored in Catholic traditions. Yet, as time has passed, these local traditions have transformed, becoming more welcoming and community-oriented, with a strong emphasis on sharing meals and festivities. Below are some customs and traditions only New Orleans locals can understand:

1. Mondays are for red beans and rice

Before the widespread use of washing machines, Mondays were designated as "laundry day" in New Orleans, which meant that ingenious housewives had little time for cooking since they had to wash every article of clothing by hand. Something that could cook on its own had to be the dinner. So, they soaked the kidney beans overnight the night before, drained them, and cooked them on the stove for the entire day before adding spices and the "trinity" of peppers, onions, and celery. Incorporating a bay leaf and a ham bone to enhance the flavour of the beans is another custom. Many still include tasso ham or andouille sausage. Although it's no longer required to do laundry on Mondays, the custom of serving red beans and rice is still in place. This dish is simple, affordable, tasty, and common in restaurants and homes; on occasion, you can even get it for free in a dive bar, particularly on Monday nights when the New Orleans Saints are playing football.

2. Mardi Gras and Carnival

During Carnival season, New Orleanians get together annually to celebrate. Thousands upon thousands of people flock to the city for the season's festivities, parades, street parties, concerts, and other special events, which end on Fat Tuesday, also known as Mardi Gras. In anticipation of the "fasting season" of Lent, which is based on Catholic customs and history, the season is full of humour and celebration. In addition, costumes are greatly encouraged, and while there is a feeling of chaos and mischief, it is also a highly structured opportunity to showcase one's deep creativity. Krewes, or "social organizations" associated with carnivals, work hard for months before the festival even begins, creating and decorating extravagant costumes, organizing parades, and building floats. Although outsiders may think this period is fleeting, New Orleanians are actively preparing for the magnificent celebration all year long. Ash Wednesday and Lent, a time for introspection and repentance until Easter, come after the event.

3. Funerals and Second Line Parades

In brass band parades held all around New Orleans, the "second line" is a custom. The brass band and the members of the group whose permission allows them to march make up the "main line" or "first line" of the procession. All other people are included in the "second line." This custom is often observed during weddings and other joyous events. It also functions as a joyous farewell to the departed, especially in cases when the person is a beloved musician or a well-known member of the community.

4. Lagniappe

Pronounced "lanny-yap," the term lagniappe signifies "a little something extra." In the context of a trade or exchange, it refers to little expressions of gratitude. A baker's dozen, an additional complimentary swig from your martini, or any other thoughtful act are typical examples. It comes from the Spanish Creole phrase "la yapa" (also known as "ñapa"), which means a free extra gift.

5. Dinners with Reveillon on Christmas Eve

In addition to having strong French influences, New Orleanian customs are deeply ingrained in the city's Catholic heritage. Reveillon, which comes from the French word for "awakening," elevates late-night munching to a whole new level. It was once a dinner served on Christmas Eve after midnight mass. Originally served at home as more of a family custom, it has now changed and is now offered in many restaurants around the city, often for a set fee that includes four or more dishes.

6. Car Bottoming Out on a Pothole

Granted, this is a much less imaginative and enjoyable experience than some of the others on the list, but smooth streets are a serious shortcoming in New Orleans, even while the city is wonderful. You'll probably have to swerve to avoid a pothole if you're traveling for more than ten minutes, and occasionally that doesn't work out so well. Because potholes are so common in this area, WGNO, one of the local news organizations, even included a section named "Pothole of the Day" on their "News with a Twist" show last year. Residents often come up with inventive methods to let people know about the potholes as they wait for them to be patched, sometimes even stuffing them with Mardi Gras beads.

7. "Parties" during hurricanes

Hurricane season is a challenging time to evacuate; nobody likes to spend hours stuck in sweltering cars with heavy traffic, wondering whether they will ever find anything to return to. A large number of storms also dissipate or change course before reaching landfall. As a result, we stay informed about storms via the news and stock up on non-perishable food, grill-friendly items, bottled water, and copious amounts of alcohol in case the power goes out.

After that, pals stop over so we can hole up together.

8. Snowballs during the summer

A snowball is not the same as a snow cone, which is common in the nation. Though the ideas are similar, a snowball has a much better texture. For that, we can thank Mary Hansen and Ernest. Ernest Hansen reportedly detested the "unsanitary conditions" and intended to purchase a pushcart to become a street vendor. Ever ingenious, he created a new device that precisely cut ice cubes to give them the texture of snow. After receiving the ice crusher patent in 1934, he and Mary founded Hansen's Sno-Bliz a few years later. His descendants continue to own and run the famous snowball stand, and several more snowball stands and stores employing his invented technique can be found all around the city. Snowballs are a cheap, refreshing delight that may help you through the hot, muggy summers. They are also a necessary survival tool. Order your preferred flavor and request that it be served with sweetened condensed milk for a delicious treat.

9. Super Sunday

Super Sunday, observed on the March Sunday nearest St. Joseph's Day (March 19), is a major event among the New Orleans Mardi Gras Indian tribes. They dress elaborately in handmade feathered outfits and parade around their communities on this particular day. Leading their Big Chiefs, the participating Mardi Gras Indian tribes interact with other tribes, or "gangs," and engage in ceremonial dances and chanting during the processions. Watched by grateful onlookers, each tribe and their Big Chief compete amicably to outdo the other. The African American communities in New Orleans make up the majority of the Mardi Gras Indians, despite the moniker. They march all year round, sometimes as separate tribes, but on Super Sunday, they come together to honour this illustrious past custom. The Central City area is the most well-liked meeting place to see this.

Money Saving Tips In New Orleans

You must find methods to reduce expenses and save money since New Orleans may be quite costly. You may do this in several ways while still taking in the elegance and allure of the city. Here are a few money-saving suggestions for your trip to New Orleans.

1. The New Orleans Pass offers free admission to 257 of the city's best attractions. Take advantage of the greatest tours in New Orleans and see the most famous places without paying extra. SAVE MONEY at well-liked destinations. Attraction fees totaling over $400 are included in the New Orleans Pass.

2. Stay somewhere other than the French Quarter: The central business district and the French Quarter are home to some of the priciest hotels in the city. Hotels also tend to fill up rapidly, especially during off-peak times.

3. Take public transit to go around the city. Despite its sometimes slowness, public transportation is the least expensive way to get about the city or get off the airport. Ride cans start at only $1.25. Obtain a three-day or three-day pass for $3 or $9 if you want to make several journeys.

4. Take use of the ferries: Rather than paying up to $50 for a tour, you may explore the Mississippi River by taking the canal St Ferry, which is free.

5. Make the most of happy hour: Since New Orleans is a nightlife hub, dining out can become pricey at night. However, before dark, which is often a happy hour, you may take advantage of half-price.

6. Dine like a local: Local cuisine is often excellent and reasonably priced. It is not necessary to visit upscale hotels to have a satisfying dinner; instead, dining like a local will save you a significant sum of money.

7. Go on a walking tour: Take a walking tour of the city to get a fantastic overview of New Orleans.

7 Best Hotels In New Orleans

1. Hotel Monteleone: This recognized jewel,  Hotel Monteleone, is located in the bustling core of New Orleans' French Quarter, and it is the perfect place to experience the enchanting beauty that it has. It boasts more than a century of lasting elegance and combines traditional appeal with modern luxury seamlessly. Experience the pleasure of luxurious rooms, indulge in delectable culinary creations at the world-famous Carousel Bar, and take in breathtaking views from our rooftop perch. There are devoted crew committed to creating experiences that will last a lifetime, and they will help to guarantee that your stay is nothing short of amazing. Here at Hotel

Monteleone, where illustrious history and unrivaled hospitality come together, you can completely immerse yourself in the spirit of the city.

2. Omni Royal Orleans: Relax in the center of

New Orleans' renowned French Quarter at the Omni Royal Orleans, which is situated at the junction of St. Louis Street and Royal Street. Only a short distance away from popular sites such as Bourbon Street and the streetcars of Toulouse Station, this hotel is the perfect place to unwind. Welded-iron railings and a restaurant that has won awards, Rib Room, are two of the features that make our hotel in New Orleans, Louisiana, an exquisite hideaway that has been awarded the Four

Diamond title for the last 31 years. The rooftop observation deck is a stunning space that has a bar, a hot pool, and breathtaking views of the city. The upscale rooms and suites include a combination of contemporary conveniences and traditional decor. These accommodations include French and Creole accents, as well as additional luxuries like balconies with views of the city and four-poster beds. Whether you're interested in eating, shopping, or sightseeing, Omni Royal Orleans is strategically placed for the perfect escape to The Big Easy. Let us help you create the New Orleans trip of your dreams with one of our special deals or hotel packages. At the Omni Royal Orleans, you may plan the wedding of your dreams.

3. Virgin Hotels New Orleans: Located in the vibrant Warehouse District of New Orleans,

Virgin Hotels New Orleans extends a warm welcome to both tourists and residents, skillfully fusing a love of food and drink with the vibrant music and cultural scene of the city. With two sumptuous penthouse suites, 238 chambers, and over  5,000 square feet of meeting and event space, this luxury getaway has it all. Savor a wide range of culinary treats at our various dining and drinking establishments, which include the prestigious Commons Club, a flagship restaurant, bar, and lounge; The Pool Club, a rooftop haven located on the thirteenth floor that provides stunning views of the city skyline along with cool drinks; and the quaint Funny Library Coffee Shop. Experience the must-see destinations of the city, which are just a short walk from our doorstep. These include the WWII Museum, Smoothie King Center, and the charming French Quarter.

4. Bourbon Orleans Hotel: A vibrant hotel  located in the center of the French Quarter awaits you. Reminiscent of the early 1800s, the Bourbon Orleans Hotel has French design. Being in the heart of New Orleans, next to the renowned St. Louis Cathedral, puts you in close proximity to everything the city has to offer, including fine dining, nightlife, and entertainment venues like Jackson Square's local artists and entertainers, as well as upmarket shopping on Royal Street.

5. Drury Plaza Hotels New Orleans:

 Experience true Travel Happy® moments with Drury Hotels. We understand the stresses of travel, which is why we're here to alleviate them. Let us handle the essentials so you can focus on enjoying your journey. From complimentary breakfast and Wi-Fi to evening snacks, soft drinks, popcorn, and access to business centers, workout facilities, and swimming pools – we've got you covered! Plus, every room is equipped with a microwave and refrigerator for added convenience. As a 100 percent family-owned and operated chain, we take pride in providing consistent quality across all our 150+ locations. You can count on crisp sheets, luxurious linens, and inviting surroundings for a restful night's

sleep. Unwind with a handcrafted cocktail or explore our curated selection of wine, spirits, and local craft beer at The Kitchen + Bar @ Cumberland Switch, conveniently located in the main lobby and open every evening.

6. Hotel Provincial: Situated in the heart of the

 French Quarter, The Hotel Provincial is a charming boutique hotel that has been a cherished part of the area since its inauguration in July 1961. Owned and managed by the Dupepe family, it holds a rich history. In 1959, Vernon and Eunice Dupepe acquired the site of the former French Market Ice House, which had succumbed to a fire. On this very spot, the initial segment of the hotel was erected or restored, featuring 44 rooms.

Over the years, guided by the vision of the second generation, the family expanded by acquiring and renovating several neighbouring historic buildings, transforming them into additional hotel accommodations. The final addition, the 500 building, welcomed guests in 1972, boosting the total rooms and suites to 92. Today, The Hotel Provincial continues to thrive under the management of the third generation of the Dupepe family, maintaining its legacy of warmth and hospitality in the heart of the French Quarter.

7. ONE11 Hotel: Located along the scenic  Mississippi Riverfront, adjacent to Woldenberg Park and the Audubon Aquarium, ONE11 Hotel presents a stylish and refined atmosphere infused with captivating design elements, all while honouring the vibrant sugar legacy of New Orleans. As the former hub of the city's bustling Sugar District during the late 19th and early 20th centuries, 111 Iberville has undergone a meticulous restoration journey from its industrial origins to emerge as the newest addition to the Vieux Carré, marking the first hotel opening in half a century.

5 Best Beaches In New Orleans

1. Grand Isle: Grand Isle is an outdoor adventurer's dream situated around 108 miles from New Orleans that's marketed as  "Sportsman's Paradise." This modest barrier island with a geographical area of just around 8 miles is one of the islands that lie between the Gulf of Mexico and the metropolis of New Orleans.

Fishing is a big aspect of both the Grand Isle culture and economy, and the region is noted for shrimp, fish, and oysters. The seas around the island are home to approximately 280 different kinds of fish. The island is also home to a variety of migrating birds. The only inhabited barrier island in Louisiana is Grand Isle.. Because of its position and low height, the town on the island has been ravaged by storms multiple times. It is a continuing effort to repair and regain lost land and wetlands from the sea.

Grand Isle is an angler's dream. It is believed that up to 95% of the Gulf's marine species have spent at least a little period of their lives in Louisiana. This island is also an important stop in the migratory flight route for birds flying to and from Latin America.

People visit Grand Isle all year long, but the summertime is the busiest season and brings new seasonal inhabitants and an increase in visitors. While there is always much to see and do on the island, there are 2 notable events that come every year: the Grand Isle Migratory Bird Festival in April and the Tarpon Rodeo fishing contest in July. Grand Isle offers various restaurant selections, and seafood with a Louisiana flair is a highlight. There are many alternatives for lodging on the island, from bed-and-breakfasts and motels to campgrounds at Grand Isle State Park. **Location:** Grand Isle, LA 70358, USA

2. Pontchartrain Beach: Pontchartrain Beach  stands out as the most accessible among New Orleans' beaches, conveniently located near the city's university. Despite its slightly unconventional setting nestled behind a business park, this beach boasts pristine white sands and sits merely a 15-minute drive from the city center.

Divided into four cozy coves, each spanning 500 feet wide and sheltered by artificial headlands, the water here remains shallow and tranquil, creating a haven for children to frolic and swim. Situated just 1.75 miles to the east is the New Orleans Lakefront Airport, offering the additional allure of watching private planes take off and land as you bask in the sun and unwind. **Location:** Lakeshore Dr, New Orleans, LA 70122, USA

3. Fontainebleau State Park: Fontainebleau  State Park encompasses a magnificent 2,800 acres of property on the shoreline of Lake

Pontchartrain, roughly 40 miles north of New Orleans. Once the site of a massive sugarcane plantation, it's since been turned into a multi-purpose R&R destination, all less than an hour's drive from the French Quarter via the Lake Pontchartrain Causeway.

The state park provides everything for a full array of travellers. Adventurers might come to kayak amongst the giant cypress trees. History aficionados get to understand the narrative of a half-ruined sugar mill. But there are also gorgeous beaches and picnic areas for families and leisure seekers.

The Fontainebleau State Park was only one of numerous landholdings under the hands of the eccentric French-Creole politician Bernard de Marigny. He maintained the land as a sugarcane plantation and brickyard until the early 1850s. He picked the name Fontainebleau in commemoration of the enormous stretch of woodland south of Paris — a one-time favorite of the French monarchs and aristocracy.

The Fontainebleau State Park was ultimately formed as a leisure area in 1942. It was one of the first large parks in Louisiana and a flagship of the Civilian Conservation Corps development program in the area, giving one of the early overnight campers in the state.

The Fontainebleau State Park is one of the most frequented state parks in Louisiana — and for good reason. It's got a whole lot of attractions under its sleeve, coupled with a rich historical history that's guaranteed to amuse and enthral.

Nature is the most apparent lure. You may come to walk the grassy meadows on the northern border of Lake Pontchartrain. They ultimately pour out onto a sandy shoreline that provides plenty of area for sunbathers and strollers alike. There's also a vast tangle of intriguing rivers and channels flowing off Bayou Cane in the east. Kayakers may kayak the streams to get a sense of the mossy hammocks of The South.

Located on the opposite side of the lake from New Orleans, Fontainebleau Beach boasts shallow seas, a soft lakebed, and white sand onshore. An onsite restroom block separates the beach in half - you'll find roughly 250 ft of sand on one side and 1,100 ft on the other, with more trees and boulders on the longer side. The Tammany Trace route welcomes those who want to remain on dry ground. It's an old railroad line that has since been levelled to welcome bikers and hikers. The trip is 31 miles in total, but you don't have to tackle the full length. Alternatively, pick the 1.2-mile boardwalk path that offers some lovely wetlands and bird watching areas.

The Fontainebleau State Park is very near to the town of Mandeville. To reach there, you'll need to drive across the Lake Pontchartrain Causeway. It takes roughly 50 minutes from the very core of New Orleans in regular traffic. There's no regular public transit to the location, so having a vehicle of your own is the best plan.

There's ample parking in the Fontainebleau State Park. The major area is situated beside the visitor's center near Fontainebleau Beach. You may also arrange to stay overnight in one of the luxurious cabins or plots.

It's a good idea to do that far in advance of visiting, especially if you intend to come in the busy summer season. Also, be cautious of traveling between June and October. That's the height of hurricane season in Louisiana, so the waters and weather may be harsh.

Location: 62883 LA-1089, Mandeville, LA 70448, USA

Open: Daily from 6 am to 9 pm

Phone: +1 985-624-4443

4. White Lake Sands Day Beach: White Lake  Sands Day Beach is a sandy seaside leisure area that's famous for watersports and sunbathing. Located near Enon, the recreational facility provides cold, clear, spring-fed lake water, exciting inflatables, and a white sandy beach for a day full of ideal family memories.

Millions of people go to White Lake Sands Day Beach every year to enjoy the sun. The facility provides something for everyone, including families with small children and couples wishing to chill down in the Louisiana heat. Community activities are also common, such as family reunions and youth group gatherings.

One of the finest elements of the White Lake Sands Day Beach is the beach itself, which is excellent for a family beach day. In addition to the beach, the White Lakes Sands Day Beach includes a fantastic waterpark complete with inflatable water slides, a blob bag, trampolines, and floating mats.

The facility is family-friendly and kid-focused, so you'll discover distinct sections for smaller children so that they can also swim and play securely. Other family-friendly activities are provided, including cabanas with barbecues, beach volleyball equipment, and paddleboard, kayak, and pedal boat rentals. The venue may also handle bigger groups.

White Lake Sands Day Beach takes safety extremely seriously and asks that all children under 15 years old be accompanied by an adult. Anyone who is unable to swim or minors under 12 years old must wear a life jacket at all times.

If you want to spend time outdoors, you may visit sites like Zona Quad Bike Recreation Park for enjoyable four-wheel adventures in the marshes and wetlands. Another nearby attraction is Louisiana River Adventures, an adventure tour provider that provides kayak and canoe trips on the Bogue Chitto.

Location: 52129 Sandstone Blvd, Franklinton, LA 70438, USA

Open: Tuesday–Sunday from 11 am to 7 pm (closed on Mondays)

Phone: +1 985-515-0114

5. The Coconut Beach: The Coconut Beach Sand Sports Complex has been the home of sand volleyball for the New Orleans region since it was opened in April 1988. This facility provides the best in outdoor sand fun and is just 15 minutes from the city center. One of the biggest  sand volleyball facilities in the country, Coconut Beach spans 100,000 square feet of artificial beach and has 22 courts. Every week, hundreds of players participate in leagues, events, and tournaments held at the venue, which accommodates both adults and children.

The first Coconut Beach was built on a playground owned by the New Orleans Recreation Development Commission and was made possible by a Cooperative Endeavour Agreement with the City of New Orleans. However, the Army Corps of Engineers needed the space for the new 17th Street Canal Pumping Station to be installed following Hurricane Katrina.

When land was eventually donated by the City of Kenner, the plant was moved to its present site. The complex's installation of dodgeball and sand football was made possible by the bigger land lot. The Coconut Beach Sand Sports Complex was renamed as a result of the modification.

A fantastic family facility featuring activities for both adults and kids is the Coconut Beach Sand Sports Complex. The facility has grown to be a local family favorite since it offers plenty of room for running about, plenty of parking, and even a station to wash off sandy feet after use. Additionally, there's a complete bar and grill with a quite large menu that includes vegetarian selections.

The facility offers a summer camp program for kids aged 10 to 17, a jogging club, and other adult and child leagues. There are alternatives for birthday parties and gatherings at that site.

Location: 100100 Coconut Beach Ct., Kenner, LA 70065, USA

Phone: +1 504-305-4090

Conclusion

There is more to New Orleans than meets the eye. It is a vivid, alive, breathing celebration of history, culture, and life. In addition to learning about the rich and varied legacy of its people, you may enjoy the greatest in music, gastronomy, art, and entertainment there. You may experience the allure of the French Quarter, the mystique of voodoo, and the spirit of Mardi Gras here. You may create lifelong memories there.

There is something in New Orleans for everyone, whether you are here for a week or just a weekend. Discover the recognizable sites, undiscovered treasures, and off-the-beaten-path attractions that give this city its distinct character. Savour the renowned food, which includes jambalaya, po-boys, and gumbo in addition to beignets and gumbo. You may take advantage of the exciting nightlife, which includes parades, festivals, and jazz clubs and pubs. You may take in all aspects of the culture, from plays and concerts to museums and galleries. From gardens and parks to marshes and plantations, you may explore the splendour.

There's always something to see and do in New Orleans, regardless of your preferences. This city will never get old to you. You will never want to go. You'll want to return here forever. I appreciate you taking the time to read this booklet and selecting New Orleans as your travel destination. I really hope you had a great experience and will come back soon. Let the good times roll till then, or laissez les bien temps rouler!

56424384R10075